THE MIRACLE OF 333

EVERYDAY MIRACLES TO INSPIRE YOU

KEALA GERHARD

Sundream ॐ Publishing
www.sundreampublishing.com
Photography, Cover & Graphic Design by Linda Hollatz

Printed in the United States of America

ISBN-10: 1-944669-01-9
ISBN-13: 978-1-944669-01-0

CONTENTS

INTRODUCTION
Living a Miraculous Life by Linda Hollatz

Miracles are surprising events that we cannot explain without the working intelligence of a higher divine force. When we experience miracles we feel guided, protected, and blessed. Our self-confidence and trust in all and everything is either strengthened or restored.

Keala has been living a miracle-filled life and I feel confident that when you connect with her through her stories the miracles in your life will increase. When I suggested to Keala to share her favorite 33 miracles in the form of a book I thought that this would be an entertaining read, a great promotional tool for her practice and a perfect opportunity to share her legacy with her friends, children, and grand-children.

To my surprise as I was reading, slightly editing, and formatting the text I noticed that I felt even better about myself and life. Her miracles triggered the memory of all the miracles I experienced and as I was working on her book new miracles in my life increased even more. Keala carries the frequency of Reconnective Healing, 333, which is one of my favorite healing modalities. Keala's loving personality and great sense of humor will open your heart so you can receive the Reconnective Healing and Miracle energy! With gratitude and excitement for many more miracles to manifest in all of our lives,

*Write from the heart of what you think is good
and beautiful and wondrous about the world.*

Neale Donald Walsch

Preface

When I look back I can say that for the first half of my life I wasn't aware of miracles at all. My childhood and my teenage years were filled with sadness, fear and anxiety. I grew up in Germany during the war and after the war fear and anxiety were present all the time. It was just the climate in the whole country. I expected continuously that something terrible would happen, some danger lurking around the corner. Death and destruction, bombs! Alarm in the night, the sound of airplanes, having to leave the warmth of the bed to go into the deep cellar. Being hungry, not enough... of anything. Scarcity was ever present.

But there is also another side to this. The Truth is when the opposite is also true. My grandfather loved me, the first of seven grandchildren, dearly. I grew up in his pharmacy, which was magical for me. He prepared all the medicine by himself and I helped him. I can still recall the smell of tinctures, herbs, teas and salves. I have many precious memories of playing in the woods and swimming in the river, picking apples and plums from the trees out in the fields. In November we could go into the vineyards and pick the grapes that were left. Nature was our playground. I feel very fortunate that I could experience the outdoors so unpolluted and quite peaceful and serene. We even had the roads to ourselves to play on. I don't remember cars. What a beautiful childhood in this way. I learned to appreciate and being grateful for the simple things in life. I also developed a deep love for nature and her beauty.

I can see now that life prepared me to find the miraculous in life. I was eight when the war ended and my father, who was also a pharmacist, came back and slowly life got easier. We didn't take it for granted that we had quiet nights and felt safe. I saw and felt a lot of suffering and my path was clear when I was ten and my grandfather died. I became a pharmacist and married one and the first miracles happened. We could take over one of the biggest pharmacies in Bavaria and we lived an abundant life.

I am forever grateful for the miracle of my two amazing children. Thank you for choosing me as your mom.

The biggest miracle is without a doubt that I met an enlightened master, Bhagwan Shree Rayneesh, later Osho and lived for two years in India, where I started to train with amazing therapists, mostly coming from Esalen in California. Trainings in Primal, Rebirthing, later Pastlife and Hypnosis and my own practice in Munich followed.

Being able to live for eighteen years on Maui and becoming a teacher for Huna and Ho'oponopono is another big miracle.

Finally the miracle of meeting my teacher, Dr. Eric Pearl and to find my passion and my mission to be of service and function as a catalyst for the Reconnective Healing frequencies, followed. My dream to reduce the suffering of the world came true.

If I had to summarize what I just wrote it would be that my quest to find the antidote - LOVE - for all the fear in my life and in all humankind led me to Osho and to find out was love is. From there I was guided to many teachers and mentors to deepen my understanding and ability to love, one of the highlights being the Hawaiian art of Forgiveness, Ho'oponopono.

After all this preparation Reconnective Healing found its way to me. Reconnective Healing is about falling in love with your client, becoming one with your client and healing yourself. Therefore my mission statement sounds like this:

Dear Higher Self
Help me to fulfill my purpose.
Use my talents and abilities to spread Love.
I surrender my work to you.
Help me to remember that my real work is
To LOVE the world back to Health.

I finally embrace the deep *knowing* that LOVE is the only reality. We are love and we are one and we are connected to all there is. Expect Miracles, that's what I want to inspire you to do. According to *A Course in Miracles*, "Miracles are natural. When they do not occur, something has gone wrong."

The idea to write a book about the everyday miracles that happen in my life – magical and wondrous, often astonishing, miracles – was on my mind for a long time. When I visited my daughter in California, we talked about going to Harbin Hot Springs. Harbin is one of the oldest and most beautiful springs in California. I was excited to go there with her. That's when one of these daily miracles happened and I felt inspired to start to write them down. I had already a journal that had on the cover the words "Believe in small miracles," Matthew 17:20. This quote from the bible was so perfect for my new adventure. I started on our first day at Harbin and continued later on Maui, where I lived at that time and again later in California. The more I was writing about the daily miracles and grateful for them the more they happened. Believe in miracles and they will happen for you, too. That's what I want this book to be about.

There are only two ways to live your life.
One is as though nothing is a miracle.
The other is as though everything is a miracle.

Albert Einstein

Miracle 1
Harbin Hot Springs, Room #33

May 4th, 2011

I am sitting outside my room, overlooking the valley of Harbin Hot Springs. I see the beautiful temple, the spring green trees, while listening to the sound of running water and warmed by the sun. I feel tremendously grateful for my life and the miracle that had to happen that I could be there. I live on Maui, Hawaii, and when I planned to visit my daughter Rupam, we talked about going to Harbin. It is her favorite place to relax, enjoy and recharge herself.

We wanted to rent a room and spend three days there. I am so happy to be with her and excited to go. I live on Maui for eighteen years now and we see each other very rarely. We have a very special relationship with each other since our master Osho told us that we are no longer mother and daughter but travelers on the same path. She was 18 at that time and we lived in India for two years being part of the commune. Rupam moved with Osho to America and later married there. That's why the following 30 years we never even lived on the same continent. She lived in America and I lived in Germany and later on Maui. This is one of the precious and rare times to be together.

However, suddenly it became difficult for her to decide to go. Her moon time was delayed and she expected it to happen around the time of my visit and so we almost let go of the idea entirely, which made us both really sad. But it is not a good time to be in the water. I couldn't change my flight and I asked her to call anyway, because of the room. She called and asked for Monday, May 3. The woman told her that the room #33 was available and it was on the 3rd. Floor. Rupam said immediately "I'll take it!" She knew about the number 333 and we often talked about it to be one of the most sacred numbers in existence. Later I will tell you more about the number 333 and the connection to the healing work I do.

I want to tell you, why it has to be a Monday, because miracles are often created by little details. Rupam built her own business as an herbalist with a line of products. Every weekend she is at the farmers market in Oakland and San Rafael. That means a lot of work.

Monday is her day off. She calls it her "Comatose Monday." We went to Harbin on Monday, the 3rd of May and neither got the room #33 nor a room on the 3rd floor but we came. Hallelujah and no moon time. Our precious companion in the unseen world knew and arranged this.

As you recognize the divine hand that shapes and guides your life, your love increases and the coincidences become miracles.

Unknown

Miracle 2
An Angel coming as a Tango Master

May 20th, 2011

I am back on Maui, back in the "Kingdom of Heaven"- that's how Hawaii is called- in my beautiful home on the sunny side of the island, in Maui Meadows, Kihei. Back also to my morning rituals and meditation and my beloved cards.

I love cards, especially Tarot cards and I play with them and give Readings for over forty years now. This reminds me of an amazing miracle.

One month after I arrived on Maui, in February 1994, I was already part of a team of Astrologers, Palm- and Card readers of "Miracles Bookstore" in Makawao and stayed with them for the next 8 years.

At that time it was the only bookstore on Maui and the meeting point of the esoteric scene on Maui. Cards are such an important part of my life. I own many decks and in the moment I play with the *Tao Oracle* by Ma Deva

Padma. These cards are a new approach to the I Ching.

Every morning I pull one card for the day. Today it was "Deliverance" – release-relieve-a fresh approach! It shows a young man standing on dusty and dry ground, he stretches out his arms to the sky, welcoming the rain, which is pouring on him.

I looked at the card and something in me relaxed and I wondered how "the relief and the new approach" might happen.

The day before I received a very hard hit from a master, actually a Tango master. I was participating in a Tango workshop and I wasn't at my best form at all. I was insecure, nervous and on the verge of getting a cold.

When he showed me a step I felt like a total beginner and he shouted at me "Relax, be in the moment, Tango is about being in the moment." The next time it was even harder. He told me that I am goal oriented, that I am already in the next step, that I have to
S-L-O-W DOWN.

Suddenly I became so tense that I couldn't do the simplest thing. My mind was spinning, and my body was in shock. It hit me right then and there that this was not only true about Tango, but what he said was about my life. I saw how much I was into "Doing" instead of "Being."

For 35 years I am with a spiritual master and my most important task is to be meditative, to be aware, to be "Here Now". I felt like a total failure. All these years of meditation and inner work and now this!!!!!

My poor spiritual ego screamed. Here I was, looking at the card "Deliverance" and I knew something would help me to see the blessings in all of this.

I prepared to go to the beach for my daily walk. I looked for a music tape to take with me, something uplifting and upbeat.

I opened the basket and saw the words " Arabic music for Tango" on the cassette tape. I was looking forward to the rhythmic music that would change my dark mood. I took my little walk man and went to

the beach. When I started to listen to my surprise I heard the voice of Kamala, my spiritual teacher for the last two years, channeling "The Masters" for me during an individual session. What a divine coincidence, what a miracle! I was excited and happy and knew this was the "Deliverance."

I listened to the whole tape and to all the wonderful things the masters had told me the year before and that I had almost forgotten.

They told me that I was part of the healing temples of Lemuria, Atlantis, and Egypt and I was a master Alchemist in Greece. I knew Eric Pearl, my teacher for the healing work I do in this lifetime, Reconnective Healing, from the time on Lemuria and later Atlantis. "You were quite close and you laughed a lot," they said. Don't tell Eric he will laugh a lot!!! He will make a joke of it.

After listening to the whole recording I was grateful again for my life and the lessons to be learned from yesterday. My Tango teacher was one of the angels that existence sends us from time to time to wake us up and make us humble again.

In "Conversations with God" by Neal Donald Walsh, God told him: "I have sent you nothing but angels." How wonderful to know this. Sometimes I forget and then miracles happen to remind me. Later in the day I enjoyed the healing sessions. I was more in the moment and I realized that my work gives me the opportunity to BE! How fantastic is this. How blessed am I.

I create miracles, because I look for them.

Wayne W. Dyer

Miracle 3
The Miracle with the Two Essential Oils

May 27th, 2011

I want to tell you that there was more than one miracle on this tape. Just a day before a little package had arrived with two essential oils. It was Spikenard and Rose oil. The masters had told me to use them both at the same time, one near each of the nostrils. It would enhance the pituitary gland, which would then release hormones into the body to heal. I had never heard of Spikenard oil and it wasn't easy to find. After a long time, the oils had arrived. Now some minutes into the recording I was listening to the instructions how to use them and their effect on me. Wow, that is good work my companions. When the oils arrived I wondered how I would ever find the tape again. Not only that, I had several sessions with Kamala and also have hundreds of tapes from years of working and using music in my Rebirthing workshops and sessions. Can you imagine how special this was for me? These moments are really "breath-taking." Sometimes I feel like my mind can't contain the miracle, the word "mind blowing" becomes an experience.

Miracle 4
333 - Miracles on My Cell Phone

May 28th, 2011

Do you see the numbers 111, 222, 333, 444, ... often? They are called time prompts. If you see these numbers it means you are capable of two way Spirit communication. Every time I see it, I take it as a sign that I am in connection with my Higher Self.

One morning I woke up and looked at my alarm clock and it was 3.33 am. That happened very often, but a new "miracle" happened later. Out of the blue I had the impulse to check my minutes on my cell phone. There wasn't really a reason at all to do it, but there it was: 333 used out of 450 minutes. Thank you Spirit for letting me know that I am in communication with you all the time!!!

Later in the day I came home from a long day out and had gotten myself, for the first time on Maui, a bunch of Roses. This is really a luxury on Maui, especially where I live. If you are lucky they are beautiful for three days – it is so hot here on the sunny side of Maui. I also made myself ice cream from frozen bananas, almond milk and Stevia, a healthy sweetener. That was a new recipe I had learned from my daughter.

Oh, that was so delicious and without guilt I celebrated my life and all the beauty in it. I just saw an advertisement, which depicted wine, roses and chocolate.

I created this experience of luxury and sensuality without the alcohol and the sugar. Life is really happening when you enjoy simple things with all your senses. I called my daughter to tell her the news, that I pampered myself today. "Yes, Rupam, I took your advice and it feels so good."

I closed my cell phone and it showed me the time: 3.33 pm. Now I really have to tell you the story about 333, the sacred number that has so much significance in my life.

Miracle 5
The Miracle of 222 and 444

Before I tell you the miracle of 333, I have to tell you the miracle that happened yesterday. It sounds totally crazy and I don't know if you can believe it. I am accustomed to number miracles, but this one!!!

I was driving home and had to stop at a red light. In front of me were two cars side by side. The right one had the number 222 and the left one 444. Can you believe it? Nobody could have ever arranged this. What a perfect introduction to the miracle of 333. This reminded me of a quote by Esther Hicks who channels Abraham, a group consciousness from a nonphysical dimension- when she experienced something similar with the meter in her car.

All things are possible. If the universe knocks itself out to give me something that only amuses me, what must its capability be about things that really matter.

Miracle 6
The Miracle of 333

June 6th, 2011

Three years ago a friend, who lived in my room when I was visiting my family in Germany, forgot the book *The Reconnection* by Dr. Eric Pearl. I called her three times but she never called back. I read the book and I was fascinated. I wanted a session.

I went very deep in this first session. I fell asleep two, three times into the session. I was so deeply relaxed afterwards I didn't remember any other time in my life when this happened. I can say that I never fell asleep in or even after a session. I decided then and there to learn this! Stress is the cause of every dis-ease and this is the most relaxing healing session I experienced. I know if we deeply, deeply relax, everything would heal. EVERYTHING.

I found out that Dr. Eric Pearl, who received these frequencies, which had this amazing effect on me, was coming to Europe in the fall. I decided to do the training with him. It happened to be in Hamburg, which is the birthplace of my Mom. It is beautiful.

The first miracle was that it turned out that the mother of my best friend on Maui, Linda, lived in Hamburg and was happy to welcome me in her home. Her home was only some bus stops away from the place where the training happened. Wow! Hamburg is one of the BIGGEST cities in Germany.

I enjoyed every moment of the training, every moment! It was October and I remember the days were sunny and warm, just beautiful. I was so grateful that I could do the training in Germany when I was there anyway, visiting my family and friends. October is also my birthday month. It is always a very high time for me. This time I was ecstatic. There was a feeling of coming home. That particular healing work felt so close to my heart.

The weekend was about Reconnective Healing. Then on Monday and Tuesday we learned "The Personal Reconnection" in a small group setting.

In the book " The Reconnection", Dr. Eric Pearl tells the story how he met a woman who told him about "The Keys of Enoch – The Book of Knowledge" by J.J. Hurtak. In this book it was predicted that there will be a time when our open ended acupuncture lines will be reconnected again to the gridlines of the planet and even further with the whole universe, with far away stars and even parallel planes of existence. Quote: *selected people will be reconnected to their original blueprint.*

She told him she can do it and it would cost $ 333. He thought this was too crazy and dismissed it. But he was a chiropractor at that time and his practice was close to the bookstore on Melrose Place in Los Angeles. After going to the bookstore and reading again and again about it, he finally decided to do it. It is done on two consecutive days and the woman drew lines on his body and recalibrated more than 100 points all over his body. The following night several lights went on and doors opened in his home – how more symbolic can it get.

That's when the healings started to happen. I mean AMAZING healings: People getting out of wheelchairs, hearing coming back and many other outstanding healings. The whole story of "The Reconnection" is so exciting. I couldn't stop reading the book. It is like reading a novel. Back to the "Personal Reconnection." We know that this process has the vibration of 333. Here is why I believe this.

Miracle 7
The Miracle of the Most Beautiful Number in Existence

June 7th, 2011

My beloved friend and housemate at that time, Rupa, loved to listen to interviews on the radio. One morning she came down to my room and excitedly told me the story of the last night's interview. It was about a man, labeled autistic, who could see numbers from 1 to 10.000 as visuals of beautiful landscapes and nature scenes.

When asked if he has numbers that he doesn't like so much and if he has a favorite number answered that he has 3 favorite numbers but his most favorite, meaning the most beautiful picture in his mind is 333.

Everybody has to pay 333 Dollars or Euros or other currency for the Personal Reconnection and this number is part of the process. The work has the vibration of 333 and the energy exchange is 333. Everything is energy.

Miracles are not contrary to nature,
but only contrary to what we know about nature.

Paulo Coehlo

Miracle 8
The Miracle of Meeting Linda

June 9th, 2011

You remember Linda and her mom in Hamburg? Now I want to tell you the miracle of how I met Linda.

At that time I lived in Upcountry Maui, in Kula, in a beautiful house together with friends in a community style. Downstairs we had an amazingly beautiful meditation room. It was built out into the garden. Three sides were all glass doors and windows. It was big enough for small groups of 15 to 20 people.

It happened that Shanti, a therapist that I knew from India, visited Maui and offered Family Constellations based on the work of German therapist Bert Hellinger. In a single session, a Family Constellation may reveal an unrecognized traumatic event that happened in previous generations of the family, which may cause present day problems and difficulties. Examples are the death of a mother during childbirth, the early death of a parent or sibling, suicide, war or abuse. This can be healed even if those affected now are not aware of the original event in the past. It will reveal itself in the session with the help of the therapist. Accepting the reality of the fact and forgiveness and compassion heal the wounds. In the end there is only love and acceptance and reverence for our ancestors, parents, and children.

I was very interested and asked her to come to our house to lead a family constellation for me. I knew that you choose people to represent your family and sometimes even ancestors and therefore you need quite a number of participants. I invited some friends and also Shanti brought some people who were more than ready to be part of it.

The day arrived. She came with a group of people and we all went down to the meditation room. After a short introduction I started with choosing the person who would represent my mom. I looked around and chose a young woman from Shanti's group.

The story unfolded. I will never forget the amazing dramatic event in the life of my grandmother that was revealed and that helped me to understand and deeply love and forgive my mom and in the end myself and everybody involved. Now comes the miracle:

We all went up into the living room to have some tea and snacks. I couldn't wait to find out more about the woman who I chose to represent my mother this afternoon. I guess you know already, it was Linda. Not only that she came from Hamburg, like my mom, but she was also born like my mom, in the sun sign of Cancer.

Linda's rising sign is in Virgo and my mom's South node is in Virgo.

Later Linda invited me for her family constellation and chose me as her mother and we found out that we both, her mom and me, have the exact same degree Virgo rising sign degree.

A deep friendship started on this afternoon. To this day we support each other in many ways. She became one of my very best friends. Without her I wouldn't have started this book.

This is one of the examples of what Alan Cohen in one of his books describes:

There is a powerful organization, called C. C. C. C, the Cosmic Coincidence Control Center that coordinates such events. This invisible agency arranges the meeting of any two people who need to connect for an important reason.

Miracle 9
The Miracle of 11:11

June 10th, 2011

Yesterday evening I was invited to the home of a client. She had told me that she wanted to do the next seminar with my teacher Dr. Eric Pearl to learn Reconnective Healing. We were sitting in front of the biggest TV I ever saw, like a movie screen and she opened on it the website of The Reconnection to find information on all the trainings. I am in wonder. Wow what an experience!

We are sitting on a big sofa, outside on the balcony, looking at this big screen. We hear the sound of the ocean, look out into the night sky and talk about miracles. For sure we talked about numbers and the sacred number 333 and miracles I experienced with it. And because it was about finding a seminar for Reconnective Healing I remembered the time when I did the seminar in Hamburg and the miracle I experienced with 11.11. When I arrived at the hotel and opened my suitcase and took out my little alarm clock to place it on the nightstand, the clock showed 11.11 am. Many times in the following years I saw this prompt, but this was the first time. I will never forget this moment. 1 is the number for new beginnings and it was a new beginning for me, a BIG one. 11 is a master number and means Illumination.

At this moment back at my client's home a seminar shows up on the screen on November 11th, 2011. We both hold our breath that means it is 11,11,11, three master numbers.

This is a perfect moment to tell you the story of 11:11. Many people see this number on their digital clocks much too often to be random. If you look up the numerology of 11:11, two master numbers side by side, it means Illumination: Illumination. It is the energy of the shift we are in, which is the shift from mind consciousness to heart consciousness. The message of this number is that we are in the biggest shift of all times. Illumination is the energy of this shift. That's why we call ourselves light workers.

11:11 became the nickname for the Harmonic Convergence in 1987. A woman, known as Solara, gave it this name. In 1992 she created the 11:11 Planetary Activation in which well over 144, 000 people participated worldwide. New crop circle formations are now appearing in the shape of a dumb bell and very large elevens forming an 11:11. The appearance of 11:11 is always a beneficial act of Divine Intervention and signifies our transition from separation to oneness consciousness. It is a doorway, a gate into a new reality, a new way to live, into a Greater Love. It is our pathway into the unknown.

I see 11:11 in wonderful ways, for example when I start a healing session. I like to give sessions at 11.00 AM. Sometimes, just before we go into the healing room, I look at the clock and then I see 11:11. Then I know this will be an Illumination for that person.

A coincidence is a miracle
in which God wishes to remain anonymous.

Dr. Gerald Jampolsky

Miracle 10
The Miracle of Meeting a Friend at Longs

June 12th, 2011

My daughter Rupam called me. She felt that I wasn't ok. I told her, that I felt sad and almost depressed. I was longing to be closer to her and also missing friends that I left behind when I moved half a year ago from Upcountry to the other side of Maui, to Kihei, the sunny side of the island.

I was especially sad about a friend, whom I had known for 30 years. I called her several times but she wouldn't call back. I had given her a healing session half a year ago. I had been waiting now for my exchange session for half a year. It was a facial and I wanted it very much because she is excellent. My daughter was very clear with me and said: "You are not sad. You are angry. You are pissed. You have to call her. This has to be finished." Oh my God, how true! I always tell my clients that depression is repressed anger and I missed it. For sure I was angry! I felt already better and knew what to do.

Around noon I had an appointment with a friend and therefore I decided to take the opportunity to go to the bank and post office and later to Longs, a drug store. I never do these things during this time of the day because it is so hot. But I also wanted to drive as little as possible. It felt so crazy and I just wanted to go home. It was 2.30 pm when I finally ended up at Longs.

When I paid at the cashier there comes that friend who lives on the other side of the island. We looked at each other in amazement. We hadn't seen each other in half a year. I did not even asked her how she had ended up, at this time, at Longs. Longs is a big store, she could have been anywhere in the store. What a coincidence! We could not have arranged this!

She told me that she has time now to give the session to me. Halleluja!!!! I told the story to Rupam and we both were amazed about the divine guidance in it.

I am realistic, I expect miracles.

Wayne W. Dyer

Miracle 11
The Priestess from Lemuria

June 13th, 2011

Today I woke up in a strange mood. There was fear and even a kind of panic inside me as if something terrible was going to happen. I know these feelings come from dreams and I decided to go to the ocean to walk and especially to swim in the ocean. I had learned from one of my teachers, Serge Kahili King, that Kahunas, the keepers of the secret, especially the Kahuna Kupua, the Shaman, would send their apprentice into the ocean to be cleansed from negativity. There is nothing more effective than ocean water for cleansing. Tears have the same cleansing effect on the heart.

I took my little tape recorder with me and the tape of Kamala channeling the masters was still in it. I started the tape where I had stopped it and the first words I could hear were about...FEAR!!! The Masters talked about me being a priestess in a white gown. "See her coming towards you, telling you about life on Lemuria, where we lived in such harmony with each other and nature and beauty and fear wasn't even known to us." "Remember me," she says to you. All my fears were gone and tears of gratitude ran down my face. What a wonderful message, what a miracle that I took this tape with me. Now is the time to tell you about Lemuria.

Hawaiians believe that their islands are the remnants of the continent Lemuria, also called Mu, the motherland. The island chain forms the mountain tops of a huge continent that sank about 60.000 years ago. By the way, not only the Hawaiians but also the Maori of New Zealand and the Aboriginals of Australia, have the same story about where we come from.

Lemuria is supposed to be the first large civilization of man. It lasted for many thousand of years, mainly due to its isolation. Lemuria was located around and on top of the largest mountain on earth, measured from the bottom of the Pacific Ocean to the top. That's Hawaii.

The story goes even further back. Hawaiians believe that the Lemurians came from the Pleiades, the star system called the Seven Sisters. I love this story that our ancestors came from the stars and that they are the Pleiadians. The Hawaiians even celebrate a time, in October and November, called Makali'i, the Hawaiian name for the Seven Sisters. The constellation is directly over Hawaii at that time. It is a time of ceremony, rest, play, and games. When the waters rose, the Hawaiians became sea fairing people and went to other parts of the world like New Zealand and Australia. Also the Hopi Indians and the Berber in Africa have very similar stories.

Miracle 12
Big Island, Kiki and 3:33 AM

June 21st, 2011

Yesterday I came back from a whole week on the Big Island. I am still filled with gratefulness about the wonderful time. It was the first time that I was there. It is so different than Maui.

It is the biggest island of these jewels in the middle of the Pacific, called Hawaii. It is five times bigger than Maui. It has a rather male energy, compared with Maui. It felt raw and powerful to me.

I had the fortune to be invited by a client to give Reconnective Healing sessions in her house to her friends. While she was traveling I took care of her little cat and the garden.

The house is built over the end of a gulch, surrounded on all sides by trees. It has a big garden with vegetables and lots of Papaya trees. I could walk to the ocean every evening. I could give the healing sessions out on the big and spacious Lanai, under the open sky, totally protected, private, and peaceful. What a gift from the universe!

I loved the cat even before I met her. Her name is Kiki. You have to know that they called me Kiki when I was a child. Actually I called myself Kiki. I couldn't say Christel, which is my German name, given at birth. I also never liked the name until I experienced a past life regression where I lived around Jesus. Now I know why I chose this name and like it.

Kiki and I loved each other and I spent almost all my meditative time with Kiki on my lap. I just loved every moment. It was one of the most wonderful, quiet, peaceful, and fulfilling weeks of my life until now. I know now I found a place where I can go in my imagination to feel deeply at peace and really in the moment.

Now comes the miracle. I woke up three nights in a row at 3.33 am. I always take my little alarm clock with me, wherever I go. I can light it up in the night and then I can get up or try to fall asleep again.

Since that time on the Big Island, where it happened the first time, I often wake up at 3:33 am. It is always a miraculous moment. I feel so loved by my Higher Self. I know I am not alone but guided by an invisible Higher Intelligence. Higher means the part of me that vibrates higher. This part is multidimensional. Here we live in a three dimensional world. It separates itself from us until we, with pure intent, take the hand of our Higher Self, letting ourselves be guided.

I am open to be a miracle in my own life and being a miracle in other people's life: a miracle of self-acceptance and self love.

Keala

Miracle 13
The Miracle of My First Mentor on Maui

July 21st, 2011

This morning I drove towards Wailea instead of my daily route. I stopped at Ulua Beach, where I knew a secret spot to be alone. I found a shady place right on the waters edge under trees. I put down my beach chair, bag, and towel and went for a long swim. When I came out of the water I found two beach chairs pretty close to mine. I was a little bewildered and turned my chair the other way, starting to change with the help of my big white towel. A woman came out of the ocean towards me and commented on my excellent job. "That was quite an accomplishment" she said, meaning I did a good job with the big towel to change my swim wear. She went to the beach chairs and we both sat down. After a while she turned towards me and asked me if it is ok if she did a quick phone call. I was so surprised that she asked and thanked her for her sensitivity.

She asked me if I lived here and for how long and that she wanted to call a friend, Romy, who was once the owner of Miracle's Bookstore. Now the miracle unfolded. I asked her if she also knew Dr. Elaine Willis. She did, what a miracle!!!! When I arrived in February 1994, a friend of mine from Germany had found Elaine, her therapy center and famous cleansing program. Elaine, a healer, nutritionist and family therapist was well known on the island and Veechi, my German friend, spent months at her place in Maui Meadows, on the sunny side of the island, almost Wailea. When I arrived she was still there and she invited me to come and spend a night there. I lived on the other side of the island at that time and was thrilled to come. In the morning at the breakfast table Elaine welcomed me and asked me about my work as a therapist. I told her that I am, beside other modalities, a rebirthing practitioner. It turned out that she loved Rebirthing and asked me to give her a session. She loved it and invited me to be part of her staff.

At that time I didn't know how blessed I was. She was known as very "picky" and only very few therapists got to work with and for her.

She became my first mentor on the island. Many beautiful hours in her center followed for the next years.

Her guided Sunday morning meditation in her house was one of the highlights of these first years on Maui. She was also a lover of the ancient Hawaiian teachings, called Huna. She invited the few Kahunas, who were still alive, into her home. Elaine was a very highly evolved being and

I remember her as radiant and full of light. She was 10 years older than me. I felt so grateful that she took me under her wings. Romy was her best friend. Later they lived together for a while. When I moved to Kula eight years ago, to the other side of the island, called Upcountry, I hardly saw her anymore, visited her only a few times. She was one of the most precious beings for me on the island.

When I moved back to Maui Meadows, I called her number and it was disconnected. Romy also had moved. So I could not find out where she was and or if she was still alive. I googled her name, found out that she was still alive but couldn't find her number.

There I was at the beach, sitting beside a woman and her husband, talking about Elaine and how much we loved her and missed her. What a miracle it was how we met here at this "secret" beach. A small miracle by the side: They told me that they lived in Germany, in Frankfurt, and their daughter was born there. They told me this in fluid German.

They invited me to join them that night to go to a private party, where I could meet Romy. Now I was happy that they had put their chairs so close to mine. How easily I could have missed this divinely guided meeting by not following my intuition to go to this beach.

I don't believe in miracles. I rely on them.

Unknown Author

Miracle 14
The Miracle of Miracles Bookstore in Makawao

August 10th, 2011

This is the perfect time to tell the story about my time as a Psychic Tarot Reader at Miracle's Bookstore.

During my first month on Maui, this was 1994, I went to this bookstore to meet the owner. Veechi, my German friend had told me about it and so I went to see if I could offer readings there.

At that time the owner's name was Mimi and the Bookstore was located in Makawao. It was a real esoteric one, with crystals and incense, Buddha statues and meditation music. It was the perfect surrounding for Tarot readings. It was love at first sight for me. Can you imagine the joy I felt when Mimi wanted a reading right away?

I gave her my famous "Karmic Relationship Tarot Reading," a reading with five cards, which shows the whole picture of a relationship including past life and future Karma. It gave her so much insight and clarity that I became part of a team of 14 readers for the next eight years. Yes, for eight years I was there with Astrologers,

Palm Readers and Psychics every week for an afternoon, or on Sunday mornings. I never knew that Romy had started Miracles Bookstore many years ago in Wailuku. How we are all interconnected!

These eight years turned out to be a wonderful time. It was the only bookstore on Maui. Everybody loved it. I remember how much I enjoyed the parties for our team at the owner's big and luxurious house. *There is no order in difficulty in miracles.*

One is not harder than another.
With God all things are possible. And I am one with God.
I know there are endless miracles in store for me.
I am open to receive them.

Marianne Williamson

Miracle 15
The Miracle of Kryon Channeling
in an Ancient Heiau

August 23rd, 2011

Tomorrow I will meet a family, a couple and their two teenage kids, to bring them to an ancient Heiau in the West Maui Mountains. They are coming from Germany, where they met Linda. She told them about the "Sacred Tour" that I offer, which reminds me of one of the most "unbelievable" Miracles in my life, where Linda played a big role. Since 1997 I have been a teacher for ancient Hawaiian wisdom, or Huna. I am blessed to have the permission of Lei'ohu Ryder, my Hawaiian mentor, who found this ancient temple to teach there.

Patrizia Pfister, one of the four international channels for Kryon, wanted to bring some groups to Maui. She needed some assistance with accommodations and management. She knew of Linda from one of her books.

She was delighted when Linda told her about me and the ancient Heiau and that I am also German. You have to know that Huna is very popular in Germany. Later the " Sacred Tour" was the absolute highlight of the group program. Patrizia came first by herself to have a taste what is going on here on Maui, to meet Linda and me. Later she came in October and November with 3 groups of 20 participants.

When she arrived she wanted to visit the ancient Heiau as soon as possible. I picked her up at Linda's house the next day and we drove up the mountain. We started to talk about how fortunate we are to have met through Linda and that we are both from Germany. So we asked each other where exactly we came from.

Because my hometown is so small, I always mention the next big town, which is Würzburg. Patrizia said "I also come from Würzburg, better, or rather from Bad Kissingen, which is only 15 miles from my hometown, famous for its healing waters." Here comes the miracle- hold your breath- it turned out we both come from the same town, my hometown, Hammelburg.

She lived for some years in the same street where my parents lived. Her boys went to the school where my sister was a teacher. She knew the pharmacy of my grandfather, where I grew up and the new pharmacy of my father where I learned and worked as a pharmacist.

Until today I always get goose bumps when I remember the moment when we found out about it and how we looked at each other in utter amazement. Two women from a small town in Germany, meeting on Maui to guide a group of people from Switzerland, Austria and Germany to an ancient temple, one channeling Kryon and the other teaching about ancient Hawaiian wisdom.

Later in October Kryon channeled through Patrizia that this Heiau is the most ancient temple on the planet, still from Lemuria. That made sense as in ancient times the temple was always high up in the mountain, overlooking the village. You know already that the islands are the mountaintops of the continent Lemuria.

When Patrizia channeled Kryon for the first group, visiting the Heiau, he recommended that everybody should be reconnected. So I gave healing sessions and the Personal Reconnection to everybody in the group. A miracle by the side: once in Munich I saw an announcement for a seminar with Dr. Eric Pearl and Lee Caroll, the English channel for Kryon, co-author of *The Indigo Children*.

As much as I know, Eric never joined with anybody in twenty years of teaching Reconnective Healing. There is an obvious connection between Kryon and Reconnective Healing. Did Kryon guide us together? Again, there are no accidents on this planet and you don't meet anybody by happenstance. In every encounter there is some Higher Consciousness involved. We are all moved around by a Higher intelligence, call it God, Love, Tao or the Divine, the same force that keeps the stars in their orbit and opens the bud of a flower.

Whatever occurs, I remember that miracles are possible
regardless of circumstances.
I rejoice in the miracles that happen in my life.
The only way to experience miracles
is to think in a miracle-minded way.

Marianne Williamson

Miracle 16
Three Small Everyday Miracles

August 24th, 2011

Little Gecko in My Shoe

These small miracles are as touching to me as the big ones. Today when I stepped out of my French gliding doors onto the porch - how much I love them - I wanted to slip into my outdoor shoes. Without thinking, I turned them over. I never did this before and I live here for nine months.

Out fell a tiny, little gecko and ran away. I was so grateful that I had the idea, or was given the idea to turn the shoes. It would have been quite a shocking experience for me and a very unpleasant one for the little gecko, possibly even the end of his life in paradise. Mahalo, which means thank you in Hawaiian for the guidance.

In Hawaiian culture geckos are bringers of luck and you are blessed when they choose to live in your home. Hawaiians would never kill a gecko. You have to clean after them quite a bit. They leave their traces everywhere but who cares!

Another Number Miracle

For quite some time I knew that my car was going to reach 150.000 miles. My white Toyota Tercel, which I got after my second car accident on Maui. My first one happened in Germany and was one of my greatest miracles. This Toyota is now fourteen years old and I love it, talk to it and call it my "White Horse."

Two days ago, when I drove home from the beach, the thought popped into my mind that it must happen soon. I looked at the odometer and at that moment it was 149.999. What an experience watching the meter changing to 150.000!!! exactly when I drove up to the house where I live. Who gave me the impulse to look in that second? What car angel tapped me on the shoulder to give me one more sign that I am never alone and always protected and guided?

Falling in Love with a Turtle

Today I woke up and I knew I wanted to go to Ulua beach for my morning walk and a good, long swim. On the way from the parking lot to the beach a woman told me that the visibility was great and that I will see a lot. It was already a mini miracle that she cared and talked to me. It never happened before in all these years that somebody told me about the condition of the ocean. That was a pleasant experience but soon I would understand more.

The water was crystal clear. I found myself surrounded by many fish of all colors and sizes like never before. I couldn't remember anything like this happening in the past. What a day! What an experience! I was elated, so happy and grateful! I swam far out and around a cliff and a formation of rocks and swam towards the beach on the other side of it. Suddenly I had to look to my right. There appeared to be a kind of shadow and there, not even an arm's length away from me, swam a huge turtle. It seemed to be almost as big as me. I could only fold my hands in front of my heart and say "Oh, oh, oh, I love you so much, you are so beautiful!"

It swam down slowly and elegantly then disappeared into the rocks, perhaps into a cave where it lives. It must have just taken a breath of air. And then I remembered the time, many years ago, when I lived on this side of the island, and went down to this beach almost every day. I often saw a turtle around this area. I knew it was the same turtle, that it lives here and that it knows me, too. I laughed and giggled all the way to the beach, I felt so blessed, so fortunate, so joyful! What a miracle.

One of the things we learn when we have experienced problems and then have received the miracle that solves them, is faith that miracles do happen. Every challenge is an opportunity ....for a miracle.

Marianne Williamson

Miracle 17
The Greatest Miracle of My Past

September 11th, 2011

The more I write about miracles, the more I am reminded of miracles that happened when I was young and not aware that there are no coincidences and that everything is guided and in the end turns out to be perfect.

When I look back, I can see that this miracle turned my life around by180 degree and that it helped me to change my whole life. I was 35 and married with two children, ten and eleven years old. My husband and I, both pharmacists, own one of the biggest pharmacies in Bavaria with fourteen employees.

I felt unfulfilled, especially in my work, seeing all the side effects, especially those of the newly found pharmaceutical drugs. Also I was not happy in our relationship. Woman's liberation was in full bloom. I was also excited to learn to treat my children with respect and as partners. My husband didn't want to join us in this. We had too many fights. I was thinking of leaving.

We decided to talk again to see if there was a solution. We went out for dinner to a restaurant in Munich, which is about 40 miles away from the town we live in. The first miracle was that we took his BMW instead of my little Renault. I needed gas and he had a full tank. We always took my smaller car because of parking problems in Munich. That, you will see, saved our lives.

The evening was a disaster. I felt hopeless and desperate. We left the restaurant around midnight. Because the country road was so empty, we didn't buckle up. I remember the moment when the headlights of the oncoming car came straight towards us. I saw this moment a hundred times in the following days in the hospital. I shouted NO with all my strength, out of the top of my lungs, grabbed the handle in front of me and pushed myself back. I lost consciousness and later had to be pulled out from the back of the car, which was totaled. The police found out the details of the accident.

Between the place where the car hit us – shown by the broken glass and metal – and the place, where we came to a still stand, was 30 yards. Knowing that we drove 60 miles/hour, the police could figure out that the other car must been going 90 miles/hour.

The physician told me that there was no explanation why we survived. It was as if we had hit a stone wall driving 150 miles/hour, unbuckled. I was told again and again "You should be dead." I was ten days in the hospital in complete solitude, aloneness and quietness. Because of the severe accident I was not allowed to do anything, no visitors, no talking, not even standing up to go to the bathroom. It was like a Zen retreat! I had to look at my life and I was shocked to realize that I didn't know what love was. Did I ever love somebody deeply, except my grandfather, who died when I was 10?

If I should be dead why not start anew? Why not change everything, risk everything and find out about love? Surprisingly I had only light injuries. When I left the hospital I immediately started psychotherapy and a two-year training in Carl Rogers' Client Centered Therapy (Humanistic Therapy) to become a therapist myself.

I found a wonderful therapist in Munich. I saw her twice a week for the next two years. I didn't have to lie down on a couch. Therapy had already changed a bit.

My therapy ended when I missed an appointment because I wanted to go to the Dynamic Meditation that I just had experienced in a Meditation Center outside of Munich, called Zist. This accident and my longing to find out about love was a straight path towards my spiritual master Osho, who was known at that time, 1976, as Bhagwan Shree Rajneesh.

I had just finished the two-year training in Client Centered Therapy. For the Certification it was required to participate in a therapy group. That's how I came to Zist, at that time one of the Meditation Centers of Osho. It became my second home. Exactly one year later, I was on my way to India to meet Osho and to become a Sannyasin. I became Ma Deva Mantra, divine chanting and singing. He said to me "Sound will be your way to God."

Osho was called "the Sex Guru," but for me his message was LOVE. Two years later I moved together with my daughter, now Ma Anand Rupam, "forever" to India to be with our master. We stayed for two years until Osho moved to Oregon. The commune around him and the city Rajneeshpuram began and with it many miracles for Rupam and myself. This is the most precious miracle of my life. Here I am adding a story about Buddha and what he said about finding a living master.

The Chances to Find a Living Master in Your Lifetime

Buddha told this story about finding a living master.
"Imagine there is a yoke with a single hole somewhere in one of all the oceans of planet earth. And suppose a blind sea turtle were there. It would come to the surface only once every 100 years. Now what do you suppose the chances would be that a blind turtle, coming once to the surface every 100 years, would stick his neck into the yoke with a single hole?"
And the monks answered, 'It would be very unusual, Sir, that a blind turtle coming to the surface once every hundred years would stick his neck into the yoke.'
"And just so, it is very, very rare that one can find a living master in their life time."

Miracle 18
The Miracle of Two Turtles and Finding Peace

September 15th, 2011

This morning I woke up again with a strange feeling, sad to be so far away from my daughter and my family in Germany. I went down to the beach to walk and swim, knowing that would help like countless times before.

What a blessing to live so close to the ocean. I couldn't wait to go into the water. The sea was calm like a lake very clear, just perfect to see all the colorful fish around the cliff. While swimming the thought came to mind that in this area I often see "my" turtle, but I told myself "Today you better drop the idea you can't expect anything, anyway you are not in a very peaceful mood." Feeling a little guilty.

After a while I turned around to swim back to the shore and here they were: two turtles beside each other, just exactly under me! All I could say was "Even two, oh, thank you, thank you, thank you."

One swam away rapidly but the bigger one remained close to me and came up to breathe twice, everything very slowly. The turtle seemed to be very old. His shield was greenish from algae and it swam so peaceful and very slow. I followed it out into the sea while crying out of joy the whole time.

The turtle told me to slow down, to enjoy life, to live in the moment, and not to worry. Life is so wonderful when you are at peace. Maluhia, Maluhia, Maluhia, Peace, Peace, Peace.

For two days, I listened again and again to CD's by Greg Braden "The Isaiia Effect" where he talks about the scrolls that were found near the Red Sea, written by the Essenes.

What touched me the most was that for them peace was the most valuable qualities of all. Not love, not compassion, not forgiveness. PEACE!!!!

The Essenes tell us "You have to know peace in your mind, feel the desire for peace in your heart and feel peace in your body." In the end it comes down to Love. To attain peace you have to love yourself.

What the Essenes already experienced 2500 years ago still is our greatest challenge. It is easier to love somebody else than to love yourself. What they suggest is to love God or the Divine with all your heart and soul, because God and you are one. Like Jesus told us "The Father and I are one."

By loving the Divine, God or however you call the Creative Force in the Universe, you love yourself.

Now I understood more deeply why Osho told us that he and we are just a manifestation of the Divine and that it doesn't matter if we love Jesus or Buddha or Shiva or Osho, it is all the same. It is about love. "You are Buddha, you are Christ, you are Osho, you are Bhagavan, you are God."

Miracle 19
The Moola Mantra Miracle

October 1st, 2011

I had moved from Upcountry Kula back to Maui Meadows into a house called "The Deeksha House." Deeksha or Oneness Blessing has its origin in India, where an enlightened couple, Amma and Bhagavan, live and have created the "Oneness University."

Every Monday we, the Deeksha givers and friends and guests who want to receive the Oneness blessings meet in the big living room. Sharina was leading these evenings for years, except when she was in India. Last Monday she asked me if I could start the evening. She had to come later. I was a little nervous. I had just become a Deeksha Giver but I felt she trusted me, so I said yes.
We always started the evening with some sharing and then with a ritual, called "Aarthi."

I love this short ritual done with a small oil lamp. The lamp is in your right hand and you move it in front of the big picture of Amma-Bhagavan while chanting the Moola Mantra. The Moola Mantra reminds us that we are light, a manifestation of the Divine.

After this I had to go around to each person and they would come close to the flame with the palms of their hands. "Taking" from the light and with a gentle movement caressing the aura around their face and head.

In the end we would all bow done in the direction of the picture.

Now come with me back to the beginning: I am standing in front of the big picture of Amma Bhagavan. I had to chant the Moola Mantra three times and repeat the second part three times and repeat the last three words three times. The words are:

AUM

SAT CHIT ANANDA PARABRAHMA

PURUSHOTAMA PARAMATMA

SHRI BHAGAVATI SAMETHA

SRI BHAGAVATE NAMAHA

I started to chant! I chanted the Moola Mantra three times and went BLANK! I couldn't continue. The words wouldn't come to my mind. Nobody continued. There was silence, and it seemed for a long time.

Finally somebody came to my rescue and we finished the ritual. I felt embarrassed but we gave each other Deeksha and I relaxed, but deep down I felt like a failure. Memories, memories! Here comes the miracle! Some days later we had a meeting with Sharina and she announced the newest change, coming from Bhagavan. For the Aarthi we have to chant only the Moola Mantra three times. NO repetitions! You can imagine how I laughed inside and was in wonder. What happened? For years the Moola Mantra was done with these repetitions and that week exactly marked the change.

Miracle 20
My Birthday Miracle

October 17th, 2011

Yippieh!!! I am so happy, happy, happy!!! I came to California to celebrate my birthday with my daughter Rupam. Yesterday, Sunday October 16th, on my birthday, we had been invited to visit a friend of hers, who lives in the mountains, near the Russian river.

A neighbor had asked this friend to take care of his house and dog while he was on his house on the Big Island for some weeks.

I was excited because Rupam knew the house. We both would have our own room and there was an oxygenated swimming pool, no chlorine.

When we arrived there, palm trees greeted us, and her friend showed us our rooms and – wow – everything was gorgeous. We had dinner out on the big deck overlooking the mountain.

We had veggies with goat cheese paneer, a type of Indian cheese, and noodles made out of sea weed, which I had never even heard of. On top of this delicious meal we had a desert, completely raw. A cheesecake with crust created from nuts and raspberry. This dinner felt so sensuous! Later Rupam's friend gave me a birthday gift, which she made for me: a ring with a labradorite, a stone that is said to support the person to bring higher

54

consciousness into the world. That is exactly what my work with Reconnective Healing is about.

Later we watched the sun set. What an experience for me. So different to see the sun going down over these mountains then seeing it on Maui going down over the ocean, where it is mostly dramatic. Here the sunset was so soft, such fine colors, very peachy and subtle.

We visited the garden and the swimming pool. Everything was Hawaii transported to the mountains of California. Later sitting on the big, queen size bed, I felt so rich, abundant and blessed. What a birthday!!! I slept like a baby into the next year of my life.

In the morning I had a long hot shower – outside!!! What a luxury to stand under the open sky with hot water warming your body. Yes, it's October and quite fresh already. What a glorious birthday gift to be a guest in this house.

Now comes the BIG miracle: The number of this house is 19333. No comment on the 333. However, when you add up the numbers of my birthday 10/16/1937 it comes out to 19. Yes, I am a 19/10/1 in the Tarot cards. 19 is the Sun, 10 the Wheel of Fortune and 1 is the Magician. No coincidence.

Miracle 21
The Miracle of Meeting Siddho in Harbin

October 23rd, 2011

Yeah! We are in Harbin again. That was Rupam's birthday gift to me. We decided to stay three nights. She asked for room 33 on the 3rd floor and we got it. She was so excited that we got this room. It is the "Egyptian" room and absolutely beautiful. There is a big statue in it and it has a royal atmosphere because of a bed, high on a pedestal and paintings of Egyptian women.

That morning I was sitting outside the room, drinking tea, enjoying the peaceful morning, when a very good-looking man, came up the stairs looking in my direction as if he knows me. Then he even waves his hand towards me. As he comes closer I recognize him. It is Siddho, a German friend, whom I met on Maui, where he lived when I arrived there. When I met him the first time on Maui it was almost a shock.

We had an intense, but short love affair in Poona in 1977 at the Ashram. I had just taken Sannyas, when Osho sent me into the encounter group, a ten-day-group process, where I met Siddho. This was a precious memory. He is one of the three men, besides my ex-husband, who are "unforgettable" in my life. Later we met only two or three times on Maui, because he lives in Kipahulu, beyond Hana, a long and winding way away.

There he was with his partner of many years, who invited him to Harbin as a birthday gift. His birthday was on October 6th. It is such a joy for all of us to meet here. We had dinner together and marveled at the miracle of life. Life is so magic. It gave us both an exceptional birthday gift.

Miracle 22
The Miracle of a Poem by Hafiz and a Quote by Alan Cohen

October 27th, 2011

We are a small community of seven people sharing the kitchen at the Deeksha House in Maui Meadows. The living room is for meetings and meditations and the Monday night Deeksha evening.

In the hallway outside the kitchen, there is a large bookshelf with all kinds of books that are there for everybody to enjoy. Sometimes I borrow books from there. I love, love, love books!!! Today I decided to give some back. One of it is the beautiful book of poems by Hafiz, the great Sufi Master, "The Gift."

I was very reluctant to let it go and decided to open it one last time before I gave it back. I like to open books and use them as an oracle. I closed my eyes asking my angels to guide me to a poem that would be very meaningful for me in these times of change and having to make important decisions.

I opened the book to a page and a poem and the title was:

"The Angels Know You Well"

What an amazing answer! It was exactly what I needed to relax and to feel so loved. Here is the poem for you to enjoy.

The Angels Know You Well

You have fathered a child with me.
You had your night of fun.
If you no longer want the love my
Beautiful body can yield

At least take care of that
Holy infant my Heart has become.
God, you sired an heir with me
When you gave birth to my soul.

I thought of complaining to all the angels last night
About your treatment of this "Homeless Child,"
But then I remembered they too
Have a long list of love-complaints.

Since I am back on Maui I have this feeling that my time here was coming to an end. I am ready to go where my heart is and I am scared. That morning I passed the bookshelf in my hallway and my eyes fell on a book by Alan Cohen "A deep Breath of Life." Again I opened the book for an answer and here is what I got:

"Great Spirit, I bow before the mystery of your wisdom. I quit trying to manipulate life, and trust you to keep me in my right place at the right time, meeting the right people for the right purpose. Thank you for your exquisite love."

Miracles come in Moments. Be ready and willing.

Wayne W. Dyer

Miracle 23

The Miracle of *Voice America Online Internet Radio Show* Calling Me

November 1st, 2011

Today there was a message on my answering machine that Voice America was interested in interviewing me. They found my website. I called back and the Executive Producer answered and we talked for one hour. After this hour I felt we had become friends. I knew something beautiful would come out of it. It turned out that she was looking for somebody to host a thirteen-week radio show, where guests and clients come in.

I told her that my daughter would be the ideal host. She has already so much experience with radio shows. There are nine hours of radio shows on her website. The producer said she would send me the host kit and look at Rupam's website. I know this would be the beginning of an exciting adventure.

She asked me about all the different modalities I offer. I talked about Reconnective Healing because she was personally interested.

I told her about the movie "The Living Matrix," which features Dr. Eric Pearl, healing a little boy from Cerebral Palsy in a few minutes. She asked me if I could do distant healing. Yes, for sure!!

I called Rupam and she was very excited. Now I became so much clearer about why I am so compelled to move to California. It felt like a dream. What a miracle that her assistant found my website. This radio station is one of the leading ones in the country with 2.5 million listeners.

Dear God,
May I not forget Your power,
In my life or in the world.
May your miracle
Be ever present in my mind.
May I remember that in You
There is always hope.
Amen.

Marianne Williamson

Miracle 24
The Miracle at the Thanksgiving Party

November 25th, 2011

There are so many blessings on this island of Maui. One is the Thanksgiving Party at Hassid and Panna's home "The Villa!" Hassid is the owner of an amazing Italian restaurant "Casanova" in Makawao, Upcountry. The villa is in Kula, high up the mountain road to Haleakala crater, the house of the sun. Every year all the Sannyasins, disciples of Osho, come together to celebrate Thanksgiving at that amazing beautiful house. I love it. It is very spacious and has a huge inside swimming pool, surrounded by green meadows and big flowery trees. I feel like I am in a dream when I am there. Around 150 people came. We formed a large circle around the tables with all the delicious food and every body shared what they were grateful for. The vibration was getting higher and higher, amazing what gratefulness can do.

Later, after eating the greatest variety of the most wonderful food I can imagine, we danced and danced, the energy raised higher, higher, and so much joy and laughter. Yes, Osho told us again and again "Dance your way to God"! We always have Karunesh as our DJ, what a blessing. Maybe you know him from his many CD's. He is one of the stars in the world of meditation music.
Now I was ready for the miracle!

I took a break from dancing and standing on the table with all the mouthwatering deserts, I saw my friend Gambheera, surrounded by people, talking about her recent adventure, a retreat in California!

Enthusiastically she talked about all the wonderful things you can do, the wilderness, the State Parks and how small Maui suddenly seems to be for her. "I love California, I want to move there," she exclaimed.

I listened and became more and more relaxed and a big heavy cloud disappeared from my being. In the end I hugged and kissed her and told her what it meant for me to hear this: "What a miracle that we met at the table and that you shared your story. You have no idea what happened to me. That lifted me out of fear and confusion and I know now what to do. I will move to California, to Sonoma, where Rupam lives. I want to be closer to her.

Every time I visit her we talk about it. Now is the time." One could say "What big miracle is this? Somebody loves California and this helps you to decide?" Well, Gambheera was for me the last person in the world I could imagine to want to move away from Maui. She lived on Maui for twenty years, in Huelo, the most Hawaiian part of the island, nature at its purest. She is a real "Maui girl!" She is an excellent gardener with a big vegetable and fruit garden. She was the baker for the biggest health food store on Maui for years. Now she works as a massage therapist at the Four Season, a dream finally fulfilled. She is also in a loving relationship and they live together happily. I know you get my point.

You are not a realist unless you believe in miracles.

Anvar Sadat

Miracle 25
Booking my Flight to California

December 10th, 2011

Since I decided to move I am full of energy and start filling moving boxes with my books, DVDs and tapes. One day I had the strong urge to book my flight to San Francisco. I needed an isle seat. I like to get up a lot and move around and it is a nightmare for me to sit between two people, so I felt under time pressure.

I like to talk to somebody and book my flights over the phone. Good that I did. I asked for February 28th, 2012 and the woman on the other side told me that there is a direct flight from Kahului to Oakland.

I never heard of a direct flight before. I was delighted. Also the time of departure, 1.25 pm was fantastic. I love to have time to prepare myself – I could even go for a walk on the beach before the flight. Yahoo!!!!

I love to travel and especially to be on a flight. The whole journey is a meditation for me. The moment everything is taken care of, I let go and I am in the moment, enjoying every second. Nothing to do, nowhere to go, just me and many hours to relax and to be. Osho told us how beautiful it is to meditate on an airplane because there is so much space around. He even gave us a special meditation for it.

The next miracle followed. She told me that the flight cost 20.000 miles. I didn't ask her, I was sure I didn't have a lot of miles. So I asked her how many miles I have.... 20.600 miles, she answered. 20.600! Hallelujah, goose bumps!

What a wonderful Omen. "And" she said, now excited for me – she felt my gratefulness- "you have two bags free, because you use your miles." When the time is right everything falls into place. A great beginning, I am happy and ready for more miracles.

God's Delays are not God's Denials.

Anthony Robbins

Miracle 26
The Christmas Pyramid Miracle

December 15th, 2011

I was packing and organizing, giving many things away, donating to the Salvation Army and also sharing some precious items with friends. A very cherished one is the Christmas Pyramid.

When my two children were small, we had such wonderful times celebrating the four weeks before Christmas. That time is called "Advent" in Germany. Every afternoon around teatime we would light candles, eat cookies, burn incense from frankincense and sing Christmas songs. For me it was one of the most wonderful times of the year to be with my children. I saw it as a preparation for the final celebration, Christmas Eve, which is the time when the children see the Christmas tree for the first time in Germany. Because it is cold outside and already dark we enjoyed the cozy feeling and we had lots of Christmas toys to play with. My favorite was the Christmas Pyramid. It is made of very light wood, looks like a little carousel, and the warmth of four candles brings it into motion. Little figures, like Santa Claus and children on sleighs create light and shadows on the walls of the room. My children loved it as much as I did. Last Christmas my daughter found such a pyramid in a second-hand store and sent it to me to Maui. She was so excited and happy to surprise me with it. She had to use a very big box to send it. It is very fragile and she had to use a lot of protection material. Now, moving to Sonoma, I wanted to give it to somebody who would enjoy it. I would have loved to send it, but it felt too much effort to send it. I didn't take this lightly. I really wanted to find somebody special, someone who would appreciate it as much as my children and I, back in Germany. I had no friends with little children and I tried hard to come up with an idea.

One of my very best friends, Veetkaya, came to my mind. She took a little girl, a daughter from an Indian friend, under her wings, playing with her once a week. Yes, that is the best idea. Veetkaya is German and she will appreciate something like this immensely. She will make sure that it is enjoyed and appreciated by the Indian girl as well. When I gave it to her she could not believe her eyes and told me this amazing story. One of her clients had asked Veetkaya, who works as a massage therapist, for years, if she could bring a pyramid for her from Germany. Veetkaya just couldn't do it since it is so fragile and needs so much care to bring it, sorry not possible. Here it was right in her house, delivered by me. I felt great. To make people happy was a wonderful feeling. *Whatever occurs, I remember that miracles are possible regardless of circumstances.*

I rejoice in the miracles that happen in my life.
The only way to experience miracles
is to think in a miracle-minded way.

Wayne W. Dyer

Miracle 27
Twenty-four People from Switzerland and a Dear Friend from Liechtenstein

January 15th, 2012

As you already know I am also a teacher of Huna "The Secrets of Ancient Hawaii." Some months ago a travel agency called me asking if I would be willing to teach a group of twenty-four people from Switzerland, mostly retired and elderly couples. It would be a daylong workshop and they would provide the lunch and pay $100 per person. What a fare well gift from the universe.

I talked with my mentor Lei'ohu and we decided that the energy of the heiau, where I usually teach my workshops would be too strong. Instead I found a wonderful place directly at the ocean with stone tables and wooden benches, shady trees and, very important, restrooms. It is very close to the heiau, just down at the sea. How and that I found it, is a miracle by itself. So far so good. The first challenge I managed.

What happened now is the real miracle I want to share today. I was excited about the possibility to share Huna and especially Ho'oponopono with people from Switzerland. Germany and Switzerland are very open to Huna. I had offered workshops there for many years.

But I was also nervous. The way I like to do it needs a lot of preparation and to handle twenty-four seniors who are still jetlagged and maybe know nothing about Huna and Lemuria had me feeling overwhelmed. I wanted somebody to be with me, to be by my side. But whom? All my friends are engaged in their own work. Most of them are massage therapists working in the big hotel resorts. Can you imagine the joy and happiness that I felt when a friend called to tell me that she wanted to come for four weeks to Maui and if we have a room for her? Yes, yes, yes. That friend, Sabrina, is from Lichtenstein, a tiny country, next to Switzerland.

She arrived exactly five days before the workshop and she was so happy about the idea to assist me on this day. Sabrina speaks "Switzerdütsch" something I can mostly understand but sometimes need translation. How more perfect could it be. What is so special is the fact that she came to Maui two years ago to learn about Huna and stayed for a year. We lived together in the same house, at that time, in Kula.

I never met anybody who is so in love with Hawaii and everything Hawaiian. Now I was only excited and looking forward to having fun and a really good time. Already we enjoyed the preparations. We decorated the stone tables in the park with tablecloths and flowers, fruits and nuts.

I found many beach chairs in our communal house and garage and took all my pillows with me. We arranged a large cotton bedspread on the grassy ground. We made flower leis for ourselves and also for the tour guide. I had prepared dried Ti leafs for the group so they could make their own head leis.

The big bus arrived and they came out one by one, greeted by two women, who could not wait to shower them with Aloha. It took a while until they opened up to our enthusiasm, but then it was just delightful. More and more we loved them.

How fascinating it was to find out what motivated them to travel all around the globe to come to Hawaii. We had a wonderful day. In the end we all hugged and I knew they would carry the seeds of the Aloha spirit with them home to Switzerland. And hopefully they will remember what I told them about Ho'oponopono, the forgiveness process. Everybody received a copy, hand written on beautiful paper, of the four short phrases, the essence of Ho'oponopono, the prayer formula:

I love you * I am sorry * Please forgive me * Thank you

You say these phrases to your Higher Self with the request to erase the memory in your unconscious mind that created the problem or negativity that you experience. If you want to know more about Ho'oponopono go to my website www.kealamaui.com

Miracle 28
The Flying Mattress on Highway 101

February 3rd, 2012

When it was clear that I would move to California, one miracle happened right away. My daughter called me and told me that her friend Seemo had to move and that she had to give back a bed that she got from Rupam two years ago. It was a queen size wooden frame that had six big drawers underneath, great for storing a lot of things.

And as a bonus I could have the mattress that she bought for the bed at that time. I was so grateful and happy. Rupam rented a storage space to bring it there. She, Seemo and Tunde, Rupam's husband, loaded his car with all the wooden parts and they had to transport the big, heavy queen size mattress on top of the car. All three had to sit in front of the car.

Driving on Highway 101 towards San Rafael Tunde suddenly felt some movement and heard some unfamiliar sounds. He looked into the outside rear mirror and shouted, "Shoot, the mattress is flying." Later he told us that he saw the mattress spiraling in the air and landing in the middle of the highway. He stopped on the side and Rupam and Seemo ran to the mattress. Cars were coming but could all go around. They managed to drag it to the side and over the rail. Two Mexican men had watched the whole scene and had also stopped to help. All together they put the mattress back on top of the car and fixed it again, this time more secure.

A few miles later a police car stopped them. "You must be the guys who lost a mattress on the Highway," the policeman said, standing by the window. Rupam looked him in the eye and with a voice so sweet and innocent. She said "the handle broke" in a way that he even showed signs of compassion.

Now comes the miracle. He didn't give them a ticket. Not for transporting a mattress that wasn't fixed properly and therefore putting many people's lives at stake, neither for sitting all three in the front without being buckled.

Later they told me that they talked about all the angels that came to their rescue. Tunde said again and again Keala's angels came to help. Not even the mattress got damaged, because there was a plastic cover over it. It was clean and beautiful.

Later they told me that it was especially dangerous because it all happened after a curve and the cars could see the mattress only at the last minute. But that was all about divine intervention, we call miracles.

Miracle 29
The Miracle of a European Bike

February 29th, 2012

Before I actually tell you the miracle you have to know that one of the greatest moments of happiness for me is going out into nature with my bike. The first fifteen years on Maui I visited Germany every summer to see my family and friends and to teach Huna. Besides visiting my sister and her family in Hammelburg, my hometown, I would live near Munich, in a small country village.

My friend Chantal, a teacher, was happy that I took care of her house and cats when she went to France to see her family. Whether I was in my hometown or stayed in Chantal's house, there was a bike. It was my only vehicle. I never needed a car.

Every day I would go out, rain or shine, it didn't matter. I would go to one of the many lakes to swim or even more exciting I would go on a trip to Munich.

Just some minutes from the house was the river *Isar* and I was able to ride along it and arrive in the center, in the middle of Munich, at the *Marienplatz*. It took about an hour and a half.

The whole area is called the *English Garden*. It is very beautiful and huge, one of the largest urban parks in the world. Stretching from the city center to the city limits, the path and walkways are roughly 100 miles all together.

That park is larger than *New York's Central Park*. There is so much beauty in this park. It offers many wonderful places to visit. The Chinese Tower was one of my favorite spots, also the Japanese teahouse. Back to my trip to Munich:

There was a pathway, mostly smoothly paved, going along on both sides of the river. In the shade of big trees, I happily biked along, forest on one side and the majestic *Isar* on the other side. I passed several beer gardens, where I sometimes stopped to take a break and drink a "Radler" – a mixture of beer and lemonade. "Rad" is the German word for bike. That drink contained just enough alcohol to feel relaxed but not drunk.

To make my trip as ecstatic as possible I took a walk man with me with my favorite music, so I could be "dancing on a bike." I spend countless hours in nature and with my bike I could go to places where no car could go. Imagine the same scenario in my hometown. Surrounded by vineyards, very similar to Sonoma, I could go out into the countryside on roads without ever seeing a car. I so enjoyed these adventures.

Now you maybe understand that I tried to buy a bike on Maui, especially when I lived Upcountry. There is a road, called Thompson road, where Oprah built her house, ideal for walking and riding a bike. There is almost no traffic. The first bike was beautiful. I took it up to this road and gave it back the same day. I couldn't enjoy the ride. 36 possibilities were just 33 too many for me. I was used to having three gears on my bike. I was battling the whole time with the gears and the brakes. The second time I tried a bike with less gears but the one gear I needed the most, wasn't working, so I gave up my dream to "Dance with my bike." Now comes the miracle.

On February 28, 2012, I finally arrived at the Oakland Airport and my daughter Rupam took me to Sonoma and showed me where I could stay until I found my own home. She had transformed her office into a cozy room. What a surprise!!! I was so grateful, felt so welcomed, and slept like a baby.

The next morning Rupam came in with an expression on her face that told me that there was another surprise, an even bigger surprise waiting for me. I felt like a child, standing outside the living room, waiting to go in and seeing the Christmas tree for the first time. She opened the door to the outside and there it was: a bike.

It looked completely new, shiny and blinking in the morning sun. Complete with a basket and a bell and even a number lock. Rupam told me the story how she found it. It was on Craig's list that she found this sweet elderly man who buys old European bikes and restores them. This one was made in Austria, many years ago. It has only three gears and you can use the pedals to manage the brakes.

I couldn't believe my eyes and was so grateful and so happy.
I also felt immensely relieved that I could wait with buying a car. Thank you, my precious companions in the unseen world and Rupam, who make my dream come true.

Miracle 30
Finding My New Home

March 17th, 2012

Tonight I will be sleeping in my new home on my new bed on the big famous mattress that hit Highway 101. I AM SO GRATEFUL! Yes, I can almost not believe it. I have to pinch myself. Only two weeks ago I arrived in Sonoma and now I am moving into my home. I arrived February 28th in the evening and March15th, 2012 I got the key to the home I envisioned. I know I am good at manifesting but this was a masterpiece. This is what I wrote on a piece of paper some weeks before:

To my Higher Self and all My Angels and Guides,
I intent to live in a wonderful HOME, close to Rupam, walking distance, for $1200 per month. Please guide me to the person, who owns it. I would like to do healing circles in my home and therefore it has to be spacious and look elegant and beautiful. Also I wish for peaceful surrounding with lots of nature and trees around, lots of space, a walk-in closet would be great. I need lots of possibilities to park cars on the road or in front of the house. I wish for a very open and relaxed owner so that I can do my healing, counseling and teaching at home.

That is almost word for word what I manifested. My new home is a fifteen-minute bike ride away from my daughter's home. Walking takes about 45 minutes. It is an English style Cottage and has been renovated by the owner over the course of a whole year. Everything is elegant and beautiful. There is a garden house in the back. It offers much more space than I could imagine. The surrounding is very peaceful and wherever I look out of a window or door I see trees. There is a huge lawn in front and a smaller garden in the back of the cottage. There is more parking space than I will ever need. One detail I want to mention is the "fire place" in the living room. It looks like real burning wood but is operated by gas. I love it. It is like the heart of my new home. There is one room, my session room, which has a loft with room for a full size mattress, ideal for guests. The kitchen has all new very elegant black appliances and is painted in a light avocado green. This is so special to me.

And on top of all this there is a huge palm tree in the front of the property, so that I can always remember Hawaii. I dealt with Sonoma Management and not the owner, which was excellent for me. This cottage was waiting for me. I know it. Everything is exactly what I need.

It was on Craig's list only for one week before we saw it there. They showed it for the first time on March 10th. On March 15th, I was approved.

The miracle was that when I arrived in Sonoma, for days my daughter and I had so much to share. We had such a great time and we just didn't want to go on the search for a home for me. After ten days we finally looked on Craig's list and found the website of Sonoma

Management. There was this cute cottage and a photo of a fireplace that captured our interest. We called and they showed it for the first time the next day, the rest is history. The rent is only $50 more, is this a miracle or not?

Be open to seeing miracles unfolding all around you,
in every flower, in every sunset and the ocean,
and in every person and every living being.

Miracle 31
Booking my First Event at the Yoga Studio

July 7th, 2012

Back on Maui a friend had given me the phone number of Bette, an Aryuvedic Astrologer. She told me that I "have" to connect with her. "She is wonderful," my friend told me. "She loves Hawaii and you will enjoy each other." I felt blessed to have already somebody to meet in my new hometown. I called Bette and we decided to meet and exchange sessions.

You can imagine how grateful I was to receive an Astrology Reading for my new beginning and also start to share my healing work. The miracles already started.

Bette told me that she has her office at the Yoga Community Center. She told me that it was the most beautiful Yoga studio she ever experienced. The idea to offer an introductory evening about my work crossed my mind immediately. I also felt excited about possibly teaching Huna there.

I asked Bette where it is and if I could get there with my bike. She told me that it was not very far from Whole

Foods, and that I would find it easily. I learned that Sonoma has bike pathways all around the city. You can go on your bike everywhere and, like in Munich, right into the center of the town, called *The Plaza*. From *the Plaza* I would find "Whole Foods."

On the day we had our first meeting, I started my adventure to find Whole Foods and the Yoga Community Center in a park close to my home. There was a bike path and when I met people on my way I just asked them. Sonoma is a town of 10.000. People are very open and friendly. However, there are also a lot of visitors – it is the famous wine country- and I had to ask a lot.

Finally I found Whole Foods and did my shopping. When I came out of the store two young women came towards me and without thinking I asked them if they were familiar with Sonoma and would know the Yoga Community Studio. One of the women said: "Yes, I know where it is. I can tell you. I am the OWNER."

We laughed and hugged and once again I was in awe of the power of C.C.C.C., the Cosmic Coincidence Control Center. It was a divine sign that this would be an important place for me. I had met Lisa, the owner, in a miraculous way and this made it all easier. It just happened effortlessly.

The Ayurvedic Astrology Reading with Bette was wonderful. The future looked bright. The Yoga Community was really a beautiful and spacious center. I am grateful that such a place exists in Sonoma. I talked with Lisa about an open evening to introduce

Reconnective Healing and she agreed to support it.

By the way I read in a magazine that Sonoma was chosen to be the most beautiful town in the whole United States. And that is where I ended up after leaving Maui, is this another miracle or not?

*A miracle though happening through one
effects the consciousness of many.*

Amma Bhagavan

Miracle 32

Reconnective Healing on the Front Cover of
Sonoma Life Magazine

August 7th, 2012

This miracle affects my life until today and into the future. In July of 2013 a woman called and wanted to meet me. She found my business card somewhere and wanted to know if I would be ready to write an article about my work for *Sonoma Life Magazine*.

I had already started to write an article for one of the newspapers– thinking that this would be a good idea - and I immediately said yes.

She gave me the email of the editor, Kevin, from that a wonderful productive and cooperative teamwork began. He was familiar with energy healing, his wife is a Reiki master and he was very open to this new and different healing modality. He interviewed me for two hours and together with what I wrote, the September issue informed their readers with four pages about Reconnective Healing.

The article included several photos of me giving Reconnective Healing to patients at the Sonoma Health

Care facility, where I used to donate my time every Wednesday. Now I tell you how the miracle unfolded.

I'll start with the photos. Kevin needed photos for the article. The first two people, who came for Reconnective Healing sessions and later became Reconnective Healing Practitioners themselves, are Mahri and Harry.

I met Harry when I had my first TV and Radio Show at the Radio Station in Sonoma. We connected the first moment we met. He called Mahri, his beloved wife, to come to see me. Mahri had her own Radio Show. She later interviewed me, and then Dr. Eric Pearl, my teacher.

Besides being the backbone of the Radio Station Harry is a filmmaker and an excellent photographer. He came to my rescue and took photos for the article. Kevin chose one of them to be on the front page of the September issue. Sonoma Life Magazine was delivered to 5000 households.

Then the October issue informed the Readers about Distant Reconnective Healing for pets. I could write the one page article.

The November issue featured Distant Healing for people on two pages with my own article and beautiful photos.

The December issue was about Huna and Ho'oponopono, the Power of Forgiveness, the Hawaiian Healing art and included over two pages with beautiful photos of my work and Hawaii. Perfect for Christmas and promoting my first workshop.

The January issue explained The Personal Reconnection on one full page with photos showing me in action. For me this complete account of the work I offered was a blessing. 25.000 people received the magazine over the last 5 months. Now comes the surprise:

This was also the last issue of *Sonoma Life Magazine*. The first issue appeared in July 2013 and the last in January 2014. Later Kevin told me "This was just for you." I had sent him Distant Healing and he had an amazing experience.

Miracle 33
My Car Angel Clayton

September 23rd, 2014

Yes, there is a red Toyota MR2 in my driveway and it was a miracle how it came to me. But today I want to share the most "angelic" miracle that ever happened to me.

I can say that this miracle gave me total trust in guidance. I see now that we are guided every step of the way. My trust in a Higher Power is rock solid. I rarely "freak out" anymore. If my precious companion in the unseen world could do THIS!!!!!! Then everything is possible for them.

Linda, who moved from Maui to California had also found a car and we blessed our cars in my driveway with a Hawaiian car blessing. In the Hawaiian way everything is alive and everything has consciousness. Since I know this I always give my car and my home and many of my possessions a name and talk to them. My car I call Vienna. This is the name of the woman who sold it to me and loved it. For my car angel I chose the name **Clayton**. Here is why.

When I arrived in Sonoma my daughter introduced me to a very special young man, whose name is **Clayton**. He is a carpenter, a gardener and also a mechanic and has many more talents. He is my "knight in shining armor."

What a blessing for a single woman. I appreciate him very much. Clayton is also open and eager to learn about Huna and Ho'oponopono, the Hawaiian teachings. He also loves Reconnective Healing and on my website you can read that he found his soul mate only six weeks after his first session. You also want to know that I live on **Clayton** Avenue. Now comes the miracle!

My new friend Joanna had invited me to come to her house, which is located outside Sonoma. She is an extraordinary woman. Not only is she an artist and a writer, but also a "chef de cuisine," an exquisite cook. She promised to prepare a meal for us and I knew this would be a piece of art. It was a Friday afternoon, around 5.00 pm and I was on my way to her home. My GPS didn't recognize the street, but she had given me directions on a piece of paper that I had taken with me. On the way I stopped and called her and she told me that there would be a difficult moment. I had to go on a highway and turn immediately left into a dirt road. Not an easy accomplishment for me, it seemed.

Later I realized that Friday 5:30 pm is the time of the highest traffic on highways anywhere. I was nervous and found myself in the middle of horrendous traffic ... and I missed the dirt road and later was on another highway to San Francisco. There was no way to turn around and the cars coming from the opposite direction lined up till the horizon, almost standing.

I pulled over to the side and called Joanna, telling her that I have to go home, that I don't know where I am and how to find my way back to her house. At that moment a car stopped in front of me and I told her "Joanna, somebody stopped and maybe can help me."

The first thing I see are bare feet. There is only one person in my world that goes barefoot most of the time and that is Clayton. And IT IS Clayton who comes towards my car and asks me if my car broke down. Until today it amazes me again and again that he was there the minute I stopped and called Joanna.

The first fact you have to know is that Clayton doesn't have a car of his own. Later he told me the story. It began with him seeing some tools on Craig's list, that he wanted to buy. He asked a neighbor if he could borrow his car. The neighbor wanted to come with him but decided otherwise. All this happened the day before. He told me the "coincidences" that had to happen for him to be there in that minute, when he recognized my car, which in itself is a miracle, and stopped.

He helped me to get back to Arnold Street where I came from and so I could start my journey again and this time Joanna had come out to the highway and was standing on it like a Joan of Arc in front of a huge truck so that I could find the entrance to the dirt road.

I was still in awe about my miracle when she told me that she asked an angel to help me to find my way to her house. You can imagine how excited I was to tell her that her prayers have been heard and that my car angel Clayton came in form of a real person.

The dinner was exquisite, her home an example of her creativity, very unique and very special. We had planned this dinner weeks ago and we looked forward to it for a long time. Finally it happened...with the help of an angel. I enjoyed her home and the wonderful food – it really was a piece of art - and the evening immensely and my heart was filled with gratitude.

Your Miracles
Collecting and Sharing the Miracles in Your Life

Did reading my Miracles remind you of Miracles that happened for you? Collecting your miracles in a diary or vision folder is an amazing practice. Anthony Robbins talks in his seminars about "Magical Moments." He creates them with his audiences. He recommends that people anchor and collect these amazing moments so that we can always connect with them through our memory and instantly feel uplifted.

Sharing your miracles only spreads good vibrations! Tell them to your loved ones or write them down for others to feel inspired.

I would love to hear your miracles.
If you would like to share them with my friends and readers, feel welcome to send me an email, so I can post them on my website.

www.kealahealing.com

Keala's Bio

The idea came to me, that instead of writing a short dry bio, I will tell you the story of my life, so that all the miracles come together like a puzzle. I can see clearly now how my life unfolded according to a divine plan.

I was born in Germany and two years old when World War II started. I grew up in my grandfather's pharmacy and I loved him dearly. He let me help him in the pharmacy, which meant a lot to me. When I was ten years old he died. It was then, when I decided to become a pharmacist.

Later, when I was 18 years old, my father, also a pharmacist, became my master and I officially learned the craft. At the university I met my husband and two children, Rupam and my son Jörn, chose us as their parents. How blessed I am. Soon after becoming pharmacists we took over one of the biggest pharmacies in Bavaria. We had fourteen employees and lived a good and happy life.

Slowly, during the following years I became more and more disappointed with the side effects of the newly created pharmaceutical drugs. In 1977, I decided to leave the pharmacy and my husband to become a therapist. That same year I went to India for two months and became a disciple of Osho, at that time called Bhagwan Shree Rajneesh. I started a two-year training in client-centered therapy in Munich.

In 1979 Rupam and I left for India and stayed until 1981 when Osho moved to Oregon, where the city of Rajneeshpuram was built. Rupam followed Osho to America and I moved to Munich.

By then I was certified as a counselor and I continued to learn bodywork, massage, Bioenergetics and Shiatsu. Rebirthing training and years of being an assistant in groups and finally leading my own groups, followed. I also studied and became certified in past life therapy, Hypnosis and NLP. Two friends and I opened our own practice in Munich called "Inner Sky."

It was such an amazing, wonderful life, but I still felt that there must be more to support my clients. That was how I was guided to find out about Huna, the ancient teachings of Hawaii. I found the missing link, the connection and communication with the Higher Self.

In 1994 I moved to Maui to study with Serge Kahili King and in 1997 I became a teacher for Huna. Later I met Kumu Hula and chanter Auli'i Mitchell, who gave me the name Keala a oli - Awakening to chanting. Kumu means teacher in Hawaiian. He believed in me and deepened my respect and my love for Hawaii and the Hawaiian Way of Life. He was my first teacher for Chanting and Hula. I also learned much from another amazing Kumu, Mahealani Henry.

I am also very grateful, that Lei'ohu Ryder offered to be my mentor and my teacher during my last years on Maui. I danced Hula for ten years under Kumu Hula Nona Kaluhiokalani in the lineage of Uncle George Naope, one of Hawaii's Living Golden Treasures. Eight years ago my life took a turn. I came across the book "The Reconnection" by Dr. Eric Pearl. When I read the book, I felt like coming home and as if I knew this teaching and philosophy from before. Today, I am very grateful to be a catalyst for this powerful Healing and that I can be of service to people and animals and the planet.

Acknowledgement
October 16th, 2017

Today is my birthday! I feel grateful and celebrate a new beginning in my life. I also celebrate the birthday of this book and its "midwife" Linda Hollatz. Linda inspired me to write this book. She was my mentor, encouraging me all the way through. She acted as my editor, publisher, photographer and graphic designer. Immense Love and Gratefulness goes to her.

Here is the story how it happened. Linda had already published several books of her own. She knew about my handwritten collection of over 100 daily miracles and my dream of writing a book. She suggested that I start to type the miracles into the computer.

"Just write every day for 33 minutes. Write 33 of your miracles until your birthday in October. On your birthday we will have a party and celebrate." Then she wrote a timeline for me with all the requirements and that kept me going. Now it is done, I kept my promise and today is my birthday and we will celebrate tonight.

I also thank my beloved daughter Rupam who patiently listened to my stories and miracles, never grew tired of them.

Thank you my son Jörn, my greatest teacher. You challenged me to grow into the person, therapist and healer that I am today.

Finally, I am grateful to my Higher Self, my guides and angels for being there for me when I needed them. This book is all about your presence in my life and my connection to you. Thank you for all the patience with me, my fears, doubts, and insecurities. "You raise me up."

I love you
I am sorry
Please forgive me
Thank you

Dear Reader,
Please understand that the information, solutions and opinions discussed in this book are offered for educational purposes only. They are not intended as diagnosis or treatment.
The use of any of this information for personal conditions should be done under the guidance of your qualified health care provider or physician.
Neither the publisher nor the author accepts responsibility for any effects that may arise from the correct or incorrect use of the information in this book.
Legal Notice: The U.S. Food and Drug Administration the health related has not evaluated the statements in this book.

www.ingramcontent.com/pod-product-compliance
Lightning Source LLC
Chambersburg PA
CBHW071622040426
42452CB00009B/1440